Madonna

Jasper Ravenwood

Madonna

Contents

1

Chapter 1: Introduction

Since the release of her eponymous debut album in 1983, Madonna has soared to the pinnacle of the music industry, becoming one of the best-selling female musicians in history. With over 300 million records sold worldwide, her influence extends beyond the mere statistics of 20 million singles sold in the UK and 58 top-10 hits. Madonna's pioneering role in transforming music into a springboard for a multimedia career, encompassing acting, writing, business, and directing, such as in the 2008 film Filth and Wisdom, is a testament to her relentless drive and vision.

Madonna's journey of self-reinvention is legendary. Over the course of her career, she has reinvented herself at least six times, earning accolades as a fashion icon. Her name still graces the marquee at exclusive couture shows, reflecting her enduring impact on the fashion world. Yet, she has also been a figure of controversy, pushing the boundaries of decency and challenging societal norms. This dichotomy—celebrated for her charitable works and criticized for her relentless pursuit of the limelight despite her advancing years—adds to her mystique.

To Madonna, controversy is not a hindrance but an essential aspect of her artistry. In a 2001 interview, she stated, "The challenge of every artist, to varying degrees, is to maintain some connection with the underground in one form or another, to try to find what is worth preserving." Her critics argue that her constant reinvention prevents her from truly connecting with the "street" and accuse her of pursuing symbolic power at any cost.

Madonna's "project" throughout her career has been a continuous reinvention, not just as a musician but as a fashion icon, actress, author, activist, and businessperson. Each of these roles will be explored in depth, revealing the complexities and contradictions that define her legacy.

2

Chapter 2: Early Life and Background

Madonna, the reigning queen of reinvention, holds the Guinness World Record for the best-selling female recording artist of all time. Her career, spanning over 35 years and decorated with seven Grammy Awards, is defined by a relentless desire to challenge the status quo. Unbound by conventional limits and often drawn to controversy, Madonna excels as a triple threat in singing, dancing, and acting, consistently positioning herself at the forefront of music and fashion.

Born Madonna Louise Ciccone on August 16, 1958, in Bay City, Michigan, she grew up in the Detroit suburb of Rochester Hills. The third of six children in a devoutly Catholic family, Madonna's upbringing was shaped by both religious discipline and creative freedom. Her father, Silvio "Tony" Ciccone, was a design engineer for Chrysler and General Motors, and her mother, Madonna Fortin, was a homemaker of French-Canadian descent. Her parents' marriage instilled in her a strong work ethic and a sense of ambition, values that would fuel her future success.

Madonna's early years were marked by a blend of traditional values and personal tragedy. In 1966, when she was just five years old, her mother passed away from breast cancer. This loss profoundly impacted her, leaving a void that she would spend much of her life trying to fill. Madonna often speaks of her mother's death as a pivotal moment that galvanized her drive and confidence. She has said, "My mother's death had a lot to do with me saying—after I got over my heartache—'I'm going to be really strong if my mother can't be. I'm going to take care of the family.' I became ambitious; I became my own little creation." This sense of responsibility and resilience became the bedrock of her relentless pursuit of success.

As a young girl, Madonna was a high achiever in both academics and extracurricular activities. She was a straight-A student and a member of the cheerleading squad. However, her true passion lay in dance. Madonna took ballet lessons from Christopher Flynn, a dance teacher who recognized her potential and encouraged her to pursue a career in dance. Flynn's mentorship provided her with the guidance and confidence she needed to follow her dreams.

In 1977, Madonna moved to New York City with a mere $35 in her pocket, determined to forge a path in modern dance. The city's pulsating energy and creative vibrancy provided the perfect backdrop for her transformation. New York in the late 1970s was a melting pot of artistic expression, and Madonna was eager to immerse herself in its cultural tapestry. She described her arrival in the city as the moment she "felt like the luckiest girl in the world." Madonna's journey was not without its hardships. She faced the challenges of living in a tough city with limited financial resources, often working low-wage jobs to make ends meet. Despite these difficulties, she remained steadfast in her pursuit of artistic excellence.

Madonna began writing songs and playing drums with "The Breakfast Club," a pop band that nurtured her nascent talents. Not long after, she also performed with the avant-garde band "Emmy." Her unique look and provocative style quickly garnered attention in the underground New York club scene. She became a regular fixture at popular clubs like Danceteria, where her bold fashion sense and electrifying performances captivated audiences. Madonna's early years in New York were a time of exploration and self-discovery. She experimented with different musical styles, collaborated with various artists, and honed her craft as a performer.

Her budding career, however, faced a significant setback in 1978 with a tragic and senseless incident. Madonna was shaken by the loss of a dear friend, who was killed in a violent attack. This personal tragedy only seemed to strengthen her resolve. Undeterred, Madonna decided to launch a solo career that same year. She reflected on this period as one of profound personal growth, saying, "I had to learn to fend for myself. It was sink or swim, and I wasn't going to let anything drag me down."

Madonna's perseverance and talent soon paid off. Her bold fashion sense, characterized by lace tops, fishnet stockings, and cross jewelry, alongside her tongue-in-cheek behavior, made her a distinctive figure in the competitive New York club scene. Her early solo gigs began to attract a growing following, setting the stage for her eventual rise to stardom. She caught the attention of music producer Mark Kamins, who helped her secure a recording contract with Sire Records.

In these formative years, Madonna's experiences in New York sculpted her artistic vision and personal identity. Her journey from a grieving young girl in Michigan to a trailblazing artist in New York is a testament to her resilience and unwavering ambition. These qualities have continued to define her career and contributions to the world of entertainment and beyond.

Madonna's early life also reflects her indomitable spirit and refusal to conform to societal expectations. She once said, "I stand for freedom of expression, doing what you believe in, and going after your dreams." This philosophy has guided her throughout her career, driving her to push boundaries and challenge norms. Whether it was her provocative performances, controversial music videos, or bold fashion choices, Madonna never shied away from expressing her individuality.

Her rise to fame in the early 1980s was meteoric. With the release of her debut single "Everybody" in 1982 and her self-titled debut album in 1983, Madonna quickly became a sensation. Her music, characterized by catchy hooks and danceable beats, resonated with a generation eager for change. Songs like "Holiday," "Lucky Star," and "Borderline" became anthems, solidifying her status as a pop icon.

Madonna's impact extended beyond music. She became a fashion trendsetter, influencing styles with her eclectic mix of punk, glam, and street fashion. Her look, often copied by fans and designers alike, became a defining feature of the 1980s. With each new album and public appearance, she continued to reinvent her image, always staying ahead of the curve.

As she ascended to global stardom, Madonna remained grounded by her early experiences and the values instilled in her by her family and mentors. Her journey from Bay City to New York and beyond is a powerful narrative of perseverance, creativity, and unyielding ambition. These qualities have not only defined her career but have also made her an enduring figure in popular culture.

3

Chapter 3: Emergence of Madonna in the Music Scene

Madonna emerged on the music scene in the early 1980s, blending a flair for fashion with an uncanny talent for knowing what would set her apart from other performers. Her early critics dismissed her as a one-hit wonder, but she has since established herself as the undisputed Queen of Pop. Known for continually reinventing both her music and her image, Madonna's contributions to music, fashion, and popular culture have left an indelible mark.

Her debut film and her subsequent releases—14 studio albums and 11 concert tours—have been vital to the British and American music industries. The sheer volume of CDs, tapes, and tickets sold attests to her immense popularity. With global sales estimated at over 300 million, Madonna ranks among the world's highest-grossing female musicians, alongside Mariah Carey, Celine Dion, and Whitney Houston. Yet, Madonna is much more than just a singer: she embodies the concept of reinvention in every sense of the term.

In the early 1980s, as the music industry was undergoing significant transformation, Madonna was crafting her unique path. Her breakthrough came with the release of her debut single "Everybody" in October 1982, which showcased her infectious energy and magnetic stage presence. The single's success led to her self-titled debut album, released in July 1983. The album featured hits like "Holiday," "Lucky Star," and "Borderline," which quickly climbed the charts and established Madonna as a rising star.

Madonna's emergence was marked by her bold fashion choices and her ability to create a distinct visual identity. She often collaborated with innovative designers and stylists to craft looks that became iconic. Her style—a mix of lace tops, fishnet stockings, and crucifix jewelry—was both provocative and trendsetting, resonating with a generation eager for new expressions of identity.

In March 1983, Madonna's face began gracing the covers of magazines, signaling her arrival on the music scene. However, her rise to fame was not without its challenges. She faced setbacks, including a canceled music video, a dancing injury at a New York City studio, and a harrowing incident that saw her being thrown over 40 feet and suffering physical abuse from an abusive boyfriend. Despite these ordeals, Madonna's resilience and determination never wavered. She found refuge and support in a homeless shelter, an experience that further fueled her resolve to succeed.

Surrounding herself with a group of loyal friends and collaborators—many of whom would become integral to her career—Madonna began to carve out her place in the industry. Her performances in New York's vibrant club scene caught the attention of influential figures, including Malcolm McLaren, the unsung svengali behind the Sex Pistols. McLaren's guidance and the connections she made in the music scene were pivotal in shaping her career.

Madonna's first major breakthrough came with the release of "When I Think of You," which shot to the top of the Hot 100 chart in April 1983. This marked her debut at number one in the United States, a feat she would replicate numerous times in the following years. Over the next 25 years, Madonna would achieve 12 chart-toppers on the Billboard Hot 100, making her the female solo artist with the most Billboard Hot 100 No. 1s.

Madonna's influence extended beyond music; she was a cultural phenomenon. Her music videos, characterized by their provocative themes and innovative choreography, became staples on MTV, further cementing her status as a pop icon. Songs like "Like a Virgin," "Material Girl," and "Like a Prayer" not only topped the charts but also sparked conversations about gender, sexuality, and societal norms.

Her ability to adapt to changing musical landscapes and reinvent herself with each album set her apart from her contemporaries. In the mid-1980s, Madonna embraced a more sophisticated sound with albums like "True Blue" and "Like a Prayer," showcasing her versatility as an artist. Her collaborations with top producers and musicians, such as Nile Rodgers, Stephen Bray, and Patrick Leonard, helped create timeless hits that remain popular to this day.

Madonna's influence was not confined to music alone. She ventured into acting, starring in films like "Desperately Seeking Susan" (1985) and "Evita" (1996), the latter earning her a Golden Globe Award for Best Actress. Her performances, while often polarizing, demonstrated her commitment to pushing artistic boundaries.

Throughout her career, Madonna has also been a trailblazer in the business world. She founded Maverick, an entertainment company, in 1992, which became a major player in the music industry. Her entrepreneurial ventures, including fashion lines, fitness centers, and children's books, further solidified her status as a multifaceted artist and businesswoman.

Madonna's emergence in the music scene was a combination of talent, tenacity, and a keen sense of timing. Her ability to tap into the cultural zeitgeist and continually reinvent herself has ensured her lasting relevance in an ever-evolving industry. As the Queen of Pop,

Madonna's legacy is one of innovation, resilience, and an unwavering commitment to her craft.

4

Chapter 4: Musical Evolution and Influences

Madonna Louise Ciccone is an artist of many layers. Though she became famous in the 1980s through her pop music and the dance club culture she helped shape, she has always been ahead of her time—a composer whose music often shines like the full moon against everyone else's dull sky. Her debut single, "Everybody," released on April 24, 1982, marked the beginning of a transformative journey that would see her continually fighting against and embracing major shifts in commercial music. Despite moments of exploitation, Madonna has always chosen to collaborate, perform, and express herself in ways she finds most meaningful. Her ability to adapt and draw from a multitude of musical genres speaks to her deep awareness of the connections between art, sexuality, politics, religion, and love—forces that resonate deeply within those who are living, breathing bodies.

Pop Music

Dubbed 'The Queen of Reinvention,' Madonna has outlasted most other influential pop stars with her creative energy and singular vision. She became an influential pop star due to her catalogue of top hits that challenged the norms of pop music, her 'girl power' approach to glamour, and her unapologetic public persona. Madonna's approach to fame, often characterized by a 'life of excess' reminiscent of the Kennedys, has made her a cultural chameleon. Today, she remains relevant for making pop music more about personal expression and less about adhering to a specific genre.

Younger generations, familiar with Madonna-influenced pop musicians like Lady Gaga, may find it surprising that Madonna was one of the first mainstream female pop musicians to push the boundaries of music and glamour unapologetically. She was among the pioneers who openly flaunted norms that relegated pop music to male sexuality and female objectification. One of Madonna's early hits was a celebration of her independence, a theme that, though normalized today, was revolutionary in the 1980s. Her declaration of female independence was a fresh perspective in pop music, and her rebellion against the beauty myth and her knack for reinvention have remained at the core of her public image for the past four decades.

Dance Music

Madonna's impact on the world of dance music is immense. Few artists can boast a slew of chart-topping hits or sell out stadiums worldwide with the ease that she does. Her music has consistently molded and been molded by the dance music scene. "Dance floor epics carried by big, big melody. That's what I thought the music of the future was," Madonna once said, succinctly describing her approach to music.

Despite a late affair with disco's resurgence through her 2005 album *Confessions on a Dance Floor*, Madonna hails from an era alternative to the club scene. Detached from her downtown New York roots, she discarded the glitterball confines when it was both fashionable and unfashionable in chart pop. This liberation allowed her to create tight, fresh, and delectable pop nuggets, bold anthems that found greater chart suitability when wrapped in dancehall, house, funk, soul, dub, or country influences. Commercially and sonically, Madonna is one of the most successful musical innovators, adept at crossing demographics and transcending clichés. Her trailblazing efforts in dance music, with hits like "Vogue" and "Into the Groove," are unforgettable. She remains a dominant force in the genre, continually influencing and being influenced by the evolving dance music landscape.

Rock and Roll

Madonna's ability to reinvent herself extends to her foray into rock and roll. Around the time of her album *Hard Candy*, she married British filmmaker Guy Ritchie and moved to England, electing to transcend traditional boundaries. Following two albums that played it safe musically and lyrically, Madonna made a conscious decision to collaborate with new producers and songwriters to craft her next album.

The result was a handful of songs inspired by her time in England, including "The Devil Wouldn't Recognize You," a biting kiss-off about her soon-to-be ex-husband, and the title track, a hip-hop-inspired dance number. Some weaker tracks came across as disingenuous attempts to break into a new genre, but *Hard Candy* ultimately demonstrated Madonna's willingness to experiment with sound, be it R&B, world music, or fluffy pop numbers for fun. The album, a mixed bag, showcases Madonna's ability to adapt and innovate within different musical genres. It serves as a reflection of her calculated risk-taking and her relentless drive to do whatever she feels passionate about, regardless of genre. She's Madonna, after all.

Evolution Over the Decades

In the mid-1980s, after releasing her self-titled debut album, Madonna transformed from the queen of New York's avant-garde scene to a global superstar. By the late 1990s, her album *Ray of Light*, released on March 3, 1998, solidified her status as a musical innovator. The album's blend of electronic music with spiritual and introspective themes resonated deeply, living at number two on the Billboard Hot 200 for four weeks. In the digital age, Madonna continued to embrace and shape new musical landscapes, working with diverse artists like Lenny Kravitz and Dave Grohl, and exploring genres like American country and African American southern-roots music in her 2012 album *MDNA*.

Madonna's musical journey over the past four decades is a testament to her ability to evolve and influence various genres. Her collaborations and experiments have included influences from Laurie Anderson's female-only New York City Drum Festival, Donna Summer's disco rhythms, and the psychedelic rock of Pink Floyd's *Dark Side of the Moon*. Albums like *Confessions on a Dance Floor* can be considered dance and house music masterpieces, while *True Blue* captures the essence of nostalgic rock and roll.

Madonna's layered artistry and her willingness to continuously reinvent herself have cemented her place as a pioneering figure in music. Her ability to blend different genres, push boundaries, and remain culturally relevant makes her one of the most enduring and influential artists of our time.

5

Chapter 5: Fashion and Style Icon

Madonna's influence in fashion is as bold and telling as her vocals. As a global figure who has arguably been more successful than any other artist in history, her catty snaps, celebrity feuds, and some seriously questionable fashion choices have played a significant part in keeping her name in headlines. Her fashion is often as notorious as her music, and her rise to the status of pop Princess is marked by her ability to constantly redefine her image and style.

Madonna has always been about change, consistently striving to reinvent her sound and image to stay new, relevant, and competitive. Many magazines have praised her for continuously changing her look and showcasing different styles that stand out, often setting trends that others quickly follow. This diversity of looks and personas, displayed since the early 1980s, is what makes Madonna an enduring fashion icon. Her name remains prominent in tabloid marquees, catwalks, and entertainment news.

Whether she's been a daring blonde or a 1950s-esque babe, Madonna has always managed to keep an unpredictable edge, worthy of a regular spread in Vivienne Westwood's creations, not to mention a commanding influence on popular culture. Over the years, she has paraded herself in rather odd combinations of clothing that have started trends, taking the world by storm. From bad girl to ballad diva, she has tried it all with chic backing. Fashion and style, therefore, remain a strong focus of Madonna's career, and her charm for all that is new and bizarre has led her into opinion-defying peculiarity. Few other stars' looks are so anxiously awaited by the hungry eyes of dedicated fans and curious critics alike.

Madonna's fashion journey can be traced back to her early days in New York City. In the 1980s, she was the epitome of street style, often seen in lace tops, fishnet stockings, and crucifix necklaces. Her iconic "Like a Virgin" wedding dress, complete with a belt that read "Boy Toy," became a defining look of the decade. This audacious combination of innocence and rebellion set the tone for many of her fashion statements to come.

As Madonna's career progressed, so did her fashion. In the 1990s, she embraced a more sophisticated and polished style, often collaborating with high-profile designers. Her infamous cone bra corset, designed by Jean-Paul Gaultier for her 1990 Blond Ambition Tour, became one of the most recognizable and talked-about pieces in fashion history. This era also saw her experimenting with a more glamorous and retro look, drawing inspiration from Hollywood's golden age.

Madonna's ability to reinvent herself continued into the 2000s and beyond. She embraced a more eclectic and edgy style, often mixing high fashion with streetwear. Her collaboration with Dolce & Gabbana for her 2010 Sticky & Sweet Tour showcased a fusion of classic Italian glamour and modern edginess. Madonna's fearless approach to fashion has always been about pushing boundaries and challenging conventions, making her a true pioneer in the industry.

Her influence extends beyond the stage and red carpet. Madonna's impact on fashion is evident in her collaborations with top designers and brands. She launched her own fashion line, Material Girl, in 2010, alongside her daughter Lourdes. The brand, aimed at young fashionistas, reflects Madonna's eclectic style and continues to be a popular choice among teens.

Madonna's style evolution has also been marked by her willingness to take risks and defy expectations. She has never been afraid to experiment with bold and unconventional looks, often blurring the lines between fashion and performance art. Whether it's her iconic red carpet appearances, her avant-garde music videos, or her stage costumes, Madonna's fashion choices always make a statement.

One of the key aspects of Madonna's fashion legacy is her ability to influence and inspire future generations. Artists like Lady Gaga, Rihanna, and Beyoncé have all cited Madonna as a major influence on their own fashion and style. Her impact on the fashion industry is undeniable, and her legacy as a style icon continues to thrive.

Madonna's fashion journey is a testament to her creativity, resilience, and unwavering commitment to self-expression. She has navigated the ever-changing landscape of fashion with grace and confidence, always staying true to her unique vision. Her ability to constantly reinvent herself and set trends has cemented her status as a fashion icon for the ages.

From her early days as a street style queen to her current status as a fashion mogul, Madonna's influence on the industry is unparalleled. Her bold and fearless approach to fashion has inspired countless individuals to embrace their own unique style and push the boundaries of what is possible. Madonna's fashion legacy is a celebration of individuality, creativity, and the power of self-expression.

6

Chapter 6: Acting Career

Madonna's acting career has been nonexclusive but highly visible. Her foray into acting began with "A Certain Sacrifice" (1979), a low-budget art film made three years earlier. While the film didn't gain much traction, it marked the start of Madonna's journey into the cinematic world. Her big-screen role as Susan, the gum-snapping "Girls just wanna have fun" singer in "Desperately Seeking Susan" (1985), was a memorable success. This film, a quirky and charming tale of mistaken identity, showcased Madonna's natural charisma and screen presence, earning her critical acclaim and a Golden Globe nomination for Best Actress in a Comedy or Musical.

However, Madonna then faced a series of box office disappointments from 1986 to 1987 with "Shanghai Surprise," "Who's That Girl," and "Bloodhounds of Broadway," the latter released the same year as "Who's That Girl." Despite the commercial failures, Madonna's commitment to her craft and her willingness to take risks were evident.

Madonna's exceptional performance in "A League of Their Own" (1992) marked a turning point in her acting career. She stole scenes as the feisty and flirtatious All the Way Mae, bringing real star quality to the role. Directed by Penny Marshall, this film about an all-female baseball league during World War II was a commercial and critical success, and Madonna's performance was widely praised.

The pinnacle of Madonna's acting career came with her portrayal of Eva Perón in the movie adaptation of Andrew Lloyd Webber and Tim Rice's musical "Evita" (1996). This role was a breathtaking career coup for Madonna, as she brought depth, emotion, and star power to the character of the iconic Argentine first lady. Her performance earned her a Golden Globe Award for Best Actress in a Motion Picture – Musical or Comedy, substantially bolstering her international gay icon status. The film's success solidified her reputation as a versatile and talented actress capable of delivering powerful performances.

Following "Evita," Madonna continued to explore various roles in film. She appeared in "The Next Best Thing" (2000), a romantic comedy-drama that received mixed reviews but showcased her ability to tackle different genres. In addition to her acting, Madonna also ventured into directing. Her directorial debut came with the 2008 film "Filth and Wisdom," a quirky comedy-drama that she also co-wrote. While the film received mixed reviews, it marked Madonna's entry into the world of filmmaking.

In 2011, Madonna directed "W.E.," a dramatic story of the affair between King Edward VIII and Wallis Simpson. This ambitious project, co-written by Madonna, aimed to explore the complexities of the controversial romance. While the film garnered mixed reviews, it demonstrated Madonna's dedication to expanding her creative horizons and her willingness to take on challenging projects.

Madonna's acting career, though marked by both successes and setbacks, highlights her relentless pursuit of artistic expression. Her ability to reinvent herself and take on diverse roles in film mirrors her approach to music and fashion. Whether she is in front of the camera or behind it, Madonna's commitment to her craft and her willingness to take risks have made her a multifaceted and influential figure in the entertainment industry.

Throughout her career, Madonna has faced criticism and praise in equal measure. Yet, her passion for storytelling and her desire to challenge herself have remained constant. Her journey from a struggling actress in low-budget films to a Golden Globe-winning performer and director reflects her resilience and determination.

Madonna's influence extends beyond her film roles. Her presence in the industry has paved the way for other musicians to transition into acting, and her bold choices have inspired many artists to explore new creative avenues. Her impact on pop culture is undeniable, and her contributions to film are a testament to her versatility and talent.

As Madonna continues to evolve as an artist, her acting career remains an integral part of her legacy. Her performances have captivated audiences, and her directorial efforts have showcased her unique vision. Madonna's journey in the world of film is a powerful reminder of her ability to transcend boundaries and redefine what it means to be an artist.

7

Chapter 7: Social and Political Activism

Madonna has been an icon for women and the LGBTQ+ community worldwide since 1985, consistently breaking barriers and challenging norms. As an activist and philanthropist, her commitment to social and environmental causes is long-standing. Unbeknownst to the world in the 1980s, she founded free clinics in the USA to combat the AIDS pandemic in a country struggling to cope with and talk about it. Self-financed, the Quinn Foundation has, over the years, provided political support, made financial contributions, and invested in projects related to AIDS and HIV in the USA, UK, Cambodia, Malawi, South Africa, and India.

In 2006, Madonna was appointed a UN Goodwill Ambassador, advocating for orphans and children in Malawi. The United Nations Secretary-General recognized her as "a global and international power, a great artist and philanthropist whose reach is global." This appointment highlighted her dedication to making a difference in the lives of those less fortunate. Her work in Malawi has been particularly impactful; she founded the nonprofit organization Raising Malawi in 2006 to support community-based programs that provide vulnerable children and orphans with health, education, and psycho-social services.

In a 1994 interview, re-analyzed in 2018, Madonna expressed her exhaustion with fame and stardom, noting that celebrities can "become the most narcissistic people on the planet, always shaking their ass and nothing else matters." This introspection marked a turning point in her public and private life. She has since focused on using her platform to advocate for the less privileged, acting as a mouthpiece to amplify the voices of marginalized communities.

Throughout her career, Madonna has used her stage performances and music videos to raise awareness about various social issues. Her work has addressed childhood trauma and abuse, homelessness, poverty, gun violence, the foster care system, and the rights of transgender communities. In her music video for "Like a Prayer," Madonna tackled themes of racism and religious intolerance, sparking both controversy and conversation. Her 2003 American Life album critiqued the American Dream and materialism, reflecting her willingness to address complex socio-political themes.

Madonna's advocacy extends beyond her artistic endeavors. She has been an outspoken supporter of LGBTQ+ rights, often using her concerts and public appearances to speak out against discrimination. In 2013, she presented the Vito Russo Award to Anderson Cooper at the GLAAD Media Awards, emphasizing the importance of fighting for equality and acceptance. Her speech at the 2019 Stonewall Inn's New Year's Eve celebration further solidified her status as a fierce ally to the LGBTQ+ community.

Her activism is not limited to social issues; Madonna has also been a vocal advocate for environmental causes. She has supported various initiatives aimed at combating climate change and promoting sustainability. In 2007, she participated in the Live Earth concert series, which aimed to raise awareness about global warming. Her commitment to environmental activism reflects her broader concern for the planet and future generations.

Madonna's influence extends to her philanthropic efforts. She has donated millions of dollars to various charities and organizations over the years. Her contributions have supported causes ranging from disaster relief to education and healthcare. Through her philanthropy, Madonna has demonstrated a deep commitment to improving the lives of people around the world.

In 2020, during the COVID-19 pandemic, Madonna continued her philanthropic efforts by donating to the Bill & Melinda Gates Foundation's Therapeutics Accelerator, which aimed to find treatments for the virus. She also supported initiatives to provide protective equipment to healthcare workers and assistance to those most affected by the pandemic.

Madonna's dedication to social and political activism has made her a role model for many. Her willingness to use her platform to advocate for change and her commitment to making a difference in the world are integral parts of her legacy. She has inspired countless individuals to take action and fight for the causes they believe in, demonstrating that one person can indeed make a significant impact.

As she continues to evolve as an artist and activist, Madonna's influence remains profound. Her ability to navigate the complex intersections of art, politics, and social justice has made her a powerful voice for change. Her legacy as an activist and philanthropist is a testament to her unwavering commitment to making the world a better place.

8

Chapter 8: Personal Life and Relationships

People close to Madonna have often referred to her as the "backbone of her family." Her father Tony described her as a stubborn child, communal, and his "little girl." After the profound loss of her mother, Madonna sought solace and support at a Kabbala Center, rekindling her spirituality and adopting the Hebrew name Esther.

Madonna lives with her four children in New York City, a place she considers home. She is a mother of six: Lourdes Leon and Rocco Ritchie, her biological children, and four adopted children from Malawi—David Banda, whom she adopted in 2006, followed by Mercy James, and twins Stella and Esther. Madonna has often spoken about the joy and fulfillment that motherhood brings her, and her commitment to her children's well-being is evident in her involvement in their lives.

Madonna's family includes her brother Christopher, who affectionately calls her Carl, while his sisters call him Chris. Christopher is a successful nightclub promoter and played a significant role in bringing Madonna into the limelight. The bond between Madonna and her siblings has had its ups and downs, but their shared history and experiences have deeply influenced her personal life.

Madonna has been married twice, first to actor Sean Penn from 1985 to 1989, and then to director Guy Ritchie from 2000 to 2008. Her marriage to Penn was marked by intense media scrutiny and tumultuous moments, but it also produced some creative collaborations, including the film "Shanghai Surprise." Her marriage to Ritchie, during which she lived in England for nearly a decade, brought a period of relative stability and resulted in the birth of their son, Rocco. Despite the eventual breakdown of both marriages, Madonna has remained amicable with both ex-husbands, emphasizing the importance of co-parenting and family.

Madonna's romantic relationships have always been a topic of public fascination. She was famously courted by rapper 2Pac after her divorce from Sean Penn, a relationship that highlighted her ability to cross cultural and social boundaries. Throughout her life, Madonna has regarded herself as bisexual and has dated women, although she is currently single.

Despite her global fame, Madonna considers New York City her home, harboring deep-rooted feelings for both the city and her fans. The energy and diversity of New York have profoundly influenced her work and identity. Although Americanized, Madonna feels a strong connection to her Italian heritage, attributing her drive and ambition to her roots. Her father Tony was born into a large Italian-American family in Iowa, and Madonna has always felt a sense of pride and connection to her family's background.

Madonna's family experiences, particularly the loss of her mother and eldest brother within two months of each other in 1966, left a lasting impression on her. These traumatic events scarred a young Madonna, shaping her resilience and determination to succeed. She attended the University of Michigan on a dance scholarship but later convinced her father to send her to New York City, where they both believed her talent and potential could be fully realized.

Madonna's personal life has always been intertwined with her career. Her relationships and experiences have often influenced her music and public persona. Despite the challenges and controversies, she has consistently shown a remarkable ability to navigate the complexities of fame while maintaining her authenticity and dedication to her craft.

Madonna's journey from a grieving young girl in Michigan to a global icon is a testament to her resilience, ambition, and unwavering commitment to her family and fans. Her personal life, marked by triumphs and tribulations, continues to inspire and captivate audiences around the world.

9

Chapter 9: Legacy and Impact on Popular Culture

As one of the most revered and influential entertainers of the 21st century, Madonna has left an undeniable footprint on Western popular culture. With over five decades of music-making and performing to her name, the "Material Girl" has accomplished innumerable feats that have left her permanently embedded in cultural memory. She serves as an archetype for reinvention, artistic maturity, and adaptation, a style icon, a purveyor of social and political commentaries, a lifestyle proprietor, and an American trailblazer in many ways.

Madonna's influence on culture is vast and multifaceted. Her ability to continuously reinvent herself has made her a symbol of adaptability and resilience. This adaptability has allowed her to stay relevant in an ever-changing industry, influencing countless artists across different genres and generations. Her innovative approach to music, fashion, and performance has set new standards and redefined what it means to be a pop star.

Madonna Studies

The academic field of "Madonna Studies" treats her work and creative output as subjects worthy of detailed study and observation.

Educators and scholars have constructed courses around her career, examining her music, videos, performances, and public persona. Given the enduring presence and intricate narrative of her image-making and her ability to foreground political and cultural concerns in her music, many claim that Madonna has become ubiquitous. Attributing an overarching blurry iconic status to her seems the most complex but inclusive and logical approach. While some artists may hide behind a veil, existing in the margins of privacy, nearly every facet of Madonna's life has been examined and discussed in the public realm.

In a sense, artists like Paul McCartney, Bono, and Michael Jackson have compelling careers, but Madonna embodies her career. Her art and life are inextricably linked, creating a unique narrative that fascinates and inspires. The overarching argument frames Madonna as a master of image recreation and re-packaging. She has morphed the Madonna image on the strength of her lead singles and promotional videos for over three decades. This mastery of image-making allows us to delve deeper into the ways she has courted the public's attention through her marriages, affairs, music, and movies.

Musical Innovation and Influence

Madonna's approaches to music, narrative-making, fashion, and album and tour marketing can be seen as reactionary. Each album era encapsulates the period while also sneaking in predictions and reflections of the times. From her early provocations with religious imagery in songs like "Like a Prayer" to her avant-garde fashion statements, Madonna's tactics are composed of a sequence of stunts meant to capture attention. She has not only influenced the music industry but has also set trends in fashion, music videos, and live performances.

Her ability to blend various musical genres and work with diverse artists has kept her music fresh and innovative. Albums like "Ray of Light" and "Confessions on a Dance Floor" showcased her willingness to experiment with electronic music and dance beats, influencing the direction of mainstream pop. Her collaborations with prominent producers and musicians have resulted in a rich and varied discography that continues to resonate with fans worldwide.

Cultural and Social Impact

Madonna's influence extends beyond music and fashion. She has consistently used her platform to address social and political issues, making her a powerful voice for change. Her work has tackled themes such as gender equality, LGBTQ+ rights, and racial justice. Her openness about her own sexuality and her support for the LGBTQ+ community have made her an icon and advocate for marginalized groups.

Her performances and music videos often serve as social commentaries, challenging societal norms and sparking important conversations. Madonna's ability to provoke thought and inspire action has solidified her status as a cultural icon. She has not only shaped the entertainment industry but has also contributed to broader cultural movements.

Legacy of Reinvention

Madonna's legacy is defined by her ability to reinvent herself. Each new era of her career brings a fresh look, sound, and message. This constant evolution has kept her at the forefront of popular culture and allowed her to maintain a strong connection with her audience. Her influence can be seen in the work of countless artists who have followed in her footsteps, from Lady Gaga to Beyoncé.

Her impact is not limited to her artistic output; Madonna has also been a trailblazer in the business world. She founded Maverick, an entertainment company, which became a major player in the music industry. Her entrepreneurial ventures, including fashion lines, fitness centers, and children's books, further demonstrate her multi-faceted talents and business acumen.

Enduring Influence

More than a quarter of a century after her initial ascendance, Madonna's impact endures. Her innovative approaches to music, fashion, and performance continue to inspire and influence new generations. She remains a powerful figure in popular culture, known for her boldness, creativity, and unwavering commitment to her artistry.

Madonna's legacy is one of innovation, resilience, and a fearless pursuit of self-expression. Her contributions to music, fashion, and social activism have left an indelible mark on the world. As future generations look back on her career, they will see a trailblazer who broke boundaries and redefined what it means to be an artist in the modern era.

10

Chapter 10: Conclusion

Whether you appreciate her or revile her, there's no denying that Madonna has had an indelible impact on American music, fashion, activism, popular culture, and ultimately, the entertainment economy and industry. For over three decades, she has fought her way to the top, reinvented herself when that no longer served her, and continually thrown the pebbles of controversy and innovation once she got there. She has broken free of, or refused to participate in, stereotypes and normalized roles, leaving a broad range of fans—gay, straight, young, and not so young—scrambling to critique, analyze, and mimic her.

Madonna is the perfect individual in so many ways. Most of us will never be, or aspire to be, Madonna, but we all have a bit of her in us. In our heart of hearts, each of us possesses the ability to change, break free from convention, exert influence, and toss a few pebbles of our own into the stagnant waters of society. Madonna is the lucrative, wildly successful, overtly outrageous representative of the person we wish we could be—the "Queen of Reinvention," without question.

Madonna's legacy is a testament to the power of self-expression and the importance of staying true to one's vision. She has shown that it is possible to navigate the complexities of fame while maintaining authenticity and using one's platform for meaningful change. Her ability to continually evolve and adapt has kept her relevant and influential across multiple generations.

Madonna's impact goes beyond her music and fashion. She has inspired countless individuals to embrace their uniqueness and to challenge societal norms. Her boldness and fearlessness have made her a role model for many, demonstrating that success is not just about talent, but also about perseverance, innovation, and the willingness to take risks.

As we reflect on Madonna's extraordinary career, it is clear that she has left an indelible mark on the world. She has transcended the boundaries of what it means to be a pop star, becoming a cultural icon and a force for change. Her legacy will continue to inspire future generations to dream big, push boundaries, and never be afraid to reinvent themselves.

In conclusion, Madonna's journey is a celebration of individuality, creativity, and the relentless pursuit of one's dreams. Her story reminds us that we all have the power to shape our destinies and make a lasting impact on the world. The "Queen of Reinvention" has shown us that change is not only possible but essential for growth and progress. Madonna's legacy will undoubtedly endure, inspiring us all to embrace our inner strength and forge our own paths.